YELLOWST[ONE]

a photographic journey

photography and text by Stephen C. Hinch

FARCOUNTRY
PRESS

Right: Foxes, while shy, are also curious. This red fox intently watched me as I photographed it from my car. I had almost given up looking for the fox when it suddenly emerged from the forest and crossed a meadow near where I was parked. After a few moments of watching each other, the fox silently trotted back toward the trees.

Far right: A thick layer of ice forms over Yellowstone Lake each winter. When and how thick the ice forms depends on how cold it gets. Usually the ice starts breaking up in early May, although the lake won't be completely free of ice until later in the month. Areas where underwater thermal features warm the water, such as at Mary Bay, will be ice-free sooner.

Title page: It takes a strong solar storm for the aurora borealis, or northern lights, to be visible in Yellowstone, but on occasion it does happen. On the night of this aurora, the best activity had waned, leaving only the green band visible in the night sky, but as luck would have it, White Dome Geyser erupted just at the moment I arrived. White Dome's eruptions only last about sixty seconds, and the exposure for the photo lasted twenty-five seconds.

Front cover: Grand Prismatic Spring is the largest hot spring in Yellowstone National Park and is a popular destination for many visitors. The spectacular color is the result of bacteria growing in different temperatures of the water. The deep clear blue water is so hot that nothing can grow there.

Back cover: Bison annually migrate to winter grazing grounds in late autumn and move back to their summer meadows in the spring. However, bison will move in large numbers at other times too. Huge herds of bison typically gather in Hayden Valley in the summer for the rut. In this photo, a huge migration was taking place as a herd of bison moved off a high plateau in February toward lower meadows. The herd stretched out for about five miles as the bison moved stoically through the snow.

ISBN: 978-1-56037-666-8

© 2017 by Farcountry Press

Photography © 2017 by Stephen C. Hinch
Text by Stephen C. Hinch

Page 17, Roosevelt Arch photograph by Jim Peaco, courtesy of the National Park Service.

For more information about our books, write Farcountry Press, P.O. Box 5630, Helena, MT 59604; call (800) 821-3874; or visit www.farcountrypress.com.

 Produced and printed in the United States of America.

22 21 20 19 18   2 3 4 5 6 7

*To my sister, Sharyn,
for her strong determination
in overcoming all the obstacles
she has encountered in her life.*

Left: Weasels are white in the winter and called ermine, but in the summer they have brown coats. This one seemed to be sizing me up as I photographed it. Weasels aren't easily seen and, since they move around so quickly, are even harder to photograph.

Far left: At 129 feet in height, Crystal Falls is largely overshadowed by the two much larger waterfalls in the Grand Canyon of the Yellowstone, Upper and Lower Falls. Many people don't even notice Crystal Falls from the Upper Falls viewing point at the Uncle Tom's parking lot. Yet a short trail leads to a wonderful viewpoint of this hidden gem.

Below: Bighorn sheep are common in Yellowstone, but given the steep terrain they call home, they can often be difficult to see. They are also sensitive to diseases carried by their domestic counterparts, and large herds of bighorns can die off from a pneumonia that is carried by domestic sheep. To get a close-up photo like this, a long telephoto lens is needed, and having the subject near a parking lot so it can be safely photographed from inside the car is ideal.

Right: The dusky grouse and sooty grouse, once thought to be the same species, are both often called blue grouse. Both can be found in the northern Rocky Mountain region and use the same habitat, and both are very pretty birds. I photographed this dusky grouse by lying on the ground with a telephoto lens to give an eye-level view while isolating the bird against the background.

Far right: The high mountain slopes of Yellowstone National Park are wonderful places to find displays of wildflowers in the middle of summer, and the cool mountain air is a nice reward when the valleys are hot. The road over Dunraven Pass provides park visitors with easy access to some of Yellowstone's beautiful high country, and an old roadbed serves as a hiking trail to the summit of Mount Washburn.

Below: Grizzlies can be seen anywhere in Yellowstone, and one should always be alert to their presence. This sow grizzly forages on vegetation while her cub, hidden in some flowers, mimics its mother's behavior. Grizzly cubs will still nurse all through the summer, but they quickly learn from their mother what is edible and what isn't—though there isn't much that isn't edible to a grizzly!

Far left: The boardwalk around Grand Prismatic Spring provides park visitors with an incredible view of the largest hot spring in Yellowstone National Park. With a diameter of 370 feet and a depth estimated at over 121 feet, it discharges roughly 560 gallons of water per minute. This photo was taken with a telephoto lens from a trail on the backside of the hot spring.

Left: Yellow columbine is the most common columbine species found in Yellowstone. It's easily distinguished by its buttery yellow petals, although sometimes part of the flower may be pink, raspberry, or white.

Below: Morning Glory Pool has long been a popular thermal feature for park visitors. Unfortunately, over the years people have thrown items into the beautiful pool, which has caused it to cool enough to lose its vivid colors. While the park service tries to clean out the items tossed in, the damage is irreparable—so please don't throw anything into any thermal feature, to help preserve them for future generations.

Above: Bison are the most common large mammal park visitors see in Yellowstone. They often appear docile but are capable of running at a top speed of thirty-five miles per hour. Park regulations require visitors to stay at least twenty-five yards from bison—but keep in mind, a bison running at top speed can cover twenty-five yards in less than 1.5 seconds! River crossings are common and can be dangerous for very young bison. But within a week or two, they are capable swimmers and can handle river crossings with ease.

Right: Cutthroat trout are found in many of the waterways in Yellowstone and spawn in small feeder streams in the summer. People can often see them during the spawning season at LeHardy Rapids on the Yellowstone River.

Far right: When travelling through the park, always keep watch for something unexpectedly dramatic. Rain clouds can give way to moody or striking theatrical lighting on scenes that otherwise might not be so interesting. That's what happened one morning while I was photographing the Yellowstone River. As the storm clouds broke, an exquisite light lit this part of the river, creating a beautiful moment I've yet to duplicate.

Far left: The village of Mammoth Hot Springs consists of the Albright Visitor Center, historic Fort Yellowstone, a clinic, the Mammoth Hot Springs Hotel and Cabins with a restaurant, employee housing, and administrative buildings. The parade ground that was used by the military in the early days still exists, though is more commonly used by elk today. This view of Mammoth Hot Springs Village was photographed from the Upper Terrace Loop Road, which is a ski trail in the winter. I enjoyed a sunset ski one evening in order to photograph this scene.

Left: When Yellowstone was established in 1872 as our first national park, there was not yet a National Park Service to preserve and protect its resources, so in 1886, the U.S. Army took on the role that the National Park Service performs today. After enduring harsh, cold winters in temporary housing, Fort Yellowstone was built at the base of Mammoth Hot Springs. Today, the buildings that originally housed military officers are now home to national park employees who are lucky enough to work in our first national park.

Below: The travertine terraces at Mammoth Hot Springs are formed from the limestone that underlies this area. Travertine is softer than the geyserite found in Yellowstone's other thermal areas, so the hot springs at Mammoth are constantly changing.

Above: A massive stone fireplace dominates the grand lobby of the Old Faithful Inn, also known as "Old House"—but it is only part of the appealing rustic ambience created by Robert Reamer's impressive log structure design.

Right: The front doors to the Old Faithful Inn were painted red, as it is the universal sign of "welcome." For first-time visitors and seasoned veterans alike, walking through those doors and seeing the Old Faithful Inn in person is a memorable experience.

Far right: The Old Faithful Inn opened in 1904 and is a National Historic Landmark. It's said to be the largest log structure in the world. For many, a trip to Yellowstone isn't complete without visiting this unique inn with a view of the most famous geyser in the world.

Above: The Roosevelt Arch was constructed in 1903. President Theodore Roosevelt was visiting at the time and was asked to place the cornerstone for the arch. For visitors using Yellowstone's north entrance at Gardiner, Montana, this is one of the first sights of Yellowstone they'll see.

PHOTO BY JIM PEACO, COURTESY OF THE NATIONAL PARK SERVICE.

Left: Old Faithful Geyser may be the most iconic image of Yellowstone National Park. The geyser erupts roughly every 74 minutes, but can range from 60 to 110 minutes, depending on the length of the last eruption. As the most famous geyser in the world, it is seen by millions of visitors each year—although few see it in the winter, especially on a minus 20 degrees morning like this.

Above: The Norris Geyser Basin is said to be the hottest and oldest geyser basin in the park and consists of two main areas: the Back Basin set in a forested area, and the Porcelain Basin painted with a rainbow of bright colors from minerals and thermophiles (miscroscopic organisms that thrive in extreme heat) and with a distinct lack of vegetation due to its hot acidic waters. Norris is forever interesting and unpredictable because its extreme environment is constantly changing. The tallest active geyser in the world, Steamboat Geyser, is found here and can erupt to heights of over 300 feet.

Right: Biscuit Basin is part of the Upper Geyser Basin, which is home to Old Faithful Geyser. It was named for biscuit-like formations seen along the edges of Sapphire Pool. In conjunction with a major earthquake in 1959, Sapphire Pool erupted, destroying the biscuit-like formations. Although it no longer resembles biscuits, the basin is still home to many pretty hot springs.

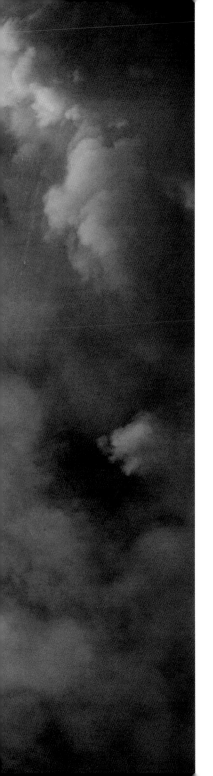

Left: Sandhill cranes are a common sight in the spring and fall as they migrate through the park. Some will stay and nest, though most move to other areas. Sandhill cranes have one of the most beautiful calls in nature, and there's nothing like hearing the call of a crane on a cool spring morning in Yellowstone. These two were seen in Hayden Valley early one morning in May.

Far left: Reaching heights of up to thirty-five feet, Sawmill Geyser is a very active geyser, and park visitors who take the time to walk the boardwalk in this area may be treated to one of its spectacular eruptions. As a fountain geyser, it bursts and splashes frequently during an eruption, and since it's close to the boardwalk, it's possible to get wet. Winter visitors should use care, as the boardwalk can be extremely icy.

Below: Winter visitors to Yellowstone will find more solitude than will summer visitors, and cross-country skiing is a popular activity. Icy boardwalks can be dangerous, but there are several well-maintained ski trails throughout the park for cross-country skiers to enjoy.

Left: A young marmot plays with an adult, possibly a parent. Marmots live in colonies with several generations of marmots sharing the same colony. They are commonly seen on the hiking trails that head up into the mountains, often sunning themselves on large boulders.

Far left: When autumn comes to Yellowstone, aspen trees will turn shades of gold and rust. During this particular autumn, these aspens in the northern part of Yellowstone were a blaze of rusty orange.

Below: As a beautiful mule deer buck paused for a moment, I was inspired to capture it with the bright autumn foliage of the cottonwood trees behind it. Mule deer are most commonly seen in the northern range of Yellowstone during the autumn, but can be seen anywhere during the summer.

Far right: Gibbon Falls is located along Grand Loop Road and is a popular roadside stop. Approximately eighty-four feet tall, the Gibbon River takes on a beautiful lacy appearance as it drops over the edge of the Yellowstone caldera. The falls and river are named after Colonel John Gibbon, who advised the 1872 Hayden Geological Expedition into Yellowstone.

Right: In 1973, the Northern Rocky Mountain gray wolf was listed on the endangered species list, and Yellowstone was selected as one of three recovery areas. In a long recovery process, wolves were reintroduced to the park in 1995 and recognized as an important predator to the Greater Yellowstone Ecosystem. They are extremely intelligent, social, and the largest of the canines. One winter day, I spotted this beautiful gray wolf as she came down a ridge and crossed the road. I photographed her from inside my vehicle using a long telephoto lens.

Below: Winters are long and all animals must endure the snow and cold. On very cold mornings, bison can be covered in frost. A frosty bison is a healthy bison, as it isn't losing heat out of its winter coat. Bison can be seen in many places in Yellowstone, even in winter. Those that stay in the thermal areas walk a fine line between using the thermals for warmth versus migrating to lower elevations where there is better winter forage.

Above: No matter how cute a grizzly and its cub may appear to be, it's always important to give them plenty of space. These two were photographed with a long telephoto lens, essential for photographing wildlife, and several park rangers were ensuring bears and people kept a safe distance from each other. When photographing the park's wildlife, always respect the rangers and listen to their instruction—it may keep you from harm and keeps the park's wildlife wild.

Left: Summer's "green" only lasts a few short months on the high-elevation plateau of Yellowstone National Park. The Gibbon River makes a picturesque resting spot on a cool summer morning, with nice opportunities for photography and fly-fishing for trout. Starting at Grebe Lake, the Gibbon River flows through Wolf Lake, then joins the Firehole River and becomes the Madison River.

Right: Long-legged American avocets can be found near Yellow-stone lakes during their migration and through summer. This handsome bird displays his rust-colored breeding plumage. The window for viewing this shorebird is usually narrow, as they only stay for a week or so before migrating south for the winter.

Far right: Sylvan Lake is a high mountain lake along the east entrance road. The lake sits just below Sylvan Pass where the road crosses the Absaroka Mountains at 8,500 feet above sea level. Top Notch Peak rises behind the lake to a height of 10,245 feet, providing a dramatic backdrop to this peaceful lake as the late afternoon sun lights the peak.

Below: Seeing a trout above water isn't easy, and neither is seeing an otter—so seeing an otter catch a trout was a wonderful surprise. When cutthroat trout spawn in the summer, otters can sometimes be spotted in the area too, as seen here at Trout Lake.

Far left: Sunset paints the sky over a meandering stream in Hayden Valley that will eventually flow into the Yellowstone River. Known as one of the best places to view wildlife in the park, especially at dawn and dusk, Hayden Valley was named for Ferdinand Hayden, an American geologist who was well known for his survey work in the Rockies in the 19th century. He led several expeditions into Yellowstone including the 1871 expedition, which provided data that was instrumental in the creation of Yellowstone National Park.

Left: While white-tailed deer are most commonly seen at lower elevations throughout the United States, mule deer, named for their large mule-like ears, are most often seen in higher elevations, like Yellowstone. However, the "muleys" will migrate out of the park in the fall and spend the winter in valleys.

Below: Recreational opportunities abound in the Yellowstone region. Camping is popular both in the park and the surrounding national forests. Just outside Yellowstone's west entrance near the town of West Yellowstone, Montana, Hebgen Lake is a popular destination for camping.

Right: Osprey arrive in Yellowstone in the spring, and many nest here. They are common near all lakes and rivers and are one of the most spotted birds of prey in the park, often seen sitting at the top of a tree overlooking the river as they wait for trout to rise.

Far right: Lost Creek Falls is a small, tranquil waterfall near Roosevelt Lodge in the northern part of Yellowstone. At only about forty feet in height, it doesn't get as much attention as its much bigger neighbors found in other parts of the park.

Below: It's rare for an elk to have twins, and these two youngsters were born playmates for each other. After playing, they both followed their mom around until it was mealtime. Raising twins is difficult for ungulates, as they must not only feed both calves but also keep both safe from potential predators.

Left: Kestrels are robin-sized birds of prey that frequent the area, though are most commonly seen in early spring when they migrate through in large numbers. This bird was photographed using a telephoto lens during the spring migration while much of the park was still covered in snow.

Far left: Riverside Geyser is often considered one of Yellowstone's most scenic geysers since it erupts in an arch over the Firehole River—and when there's a rainbow, it just adds to the grandeur of the moment! Eruptions occur about every five and a half to six and a half hours, and can reach a height of seventy-five feet.

Below: A coyote walks down a snow-covered road during the winter. Coyotes and other mammals are often easier to spot in the winter since the park is blanketed in several feet of snow, covering the sagebrush that camouflage the animals. In addition, coyotes are more active in the daylight hours of winter compared to summer due to cold temperatures and the need to find food.

Right: Sandhill cranes can be found during the warm months, but are easiest to see during the spring and autumn migrations. I spotted this crane in the autumn and its beautiful color in the golden grasses motivated me to photograph this image. Interesting behaviors, such as stretching its wings, adds to the moment.

Far right: Gibbon Meadow is a beautiful open area through which the Gibbon River flows. Surrounded by pine forest on all sides, Mount Holmes rises on the horizon, and several thermal areas can be seen in the distance. Park visitors may also see bison here.

Below: Elk enter their breeding season, or rut, in September. During this time bulls will court many cows, but the cows will refuse the males until they are ready. These two elk sharing a tender moment were photographed in Mammoth Hot Springs, one of the best places to see elk in Yellowstone.

Left: Wild cats are by far the most difficult of Yellowstone's inhabitants to see—in part, because two of the feline species, mountain lions and lynx, are not here in large numbers, but also because they are largely nocturnal in behavior and very elusive by nature. Bobcats are more common, but still very difficult to see. This bobcat was hunting waterfowl along the river's edge when I caught its image.

Far left: The terraces at Mammoth Hot Springs provide a rainbow of colors as different bacteria grow in different water temperatures. The travertine at Mammoth Hot Springs deposits quickly forming the beautiful but delicate features and providing a unique environment much different than other thermal areas in Yellowstone.

Below: Black bears can come in different colors including cinnamon, brown, or even blonde. And a black-colored black bear can have off-spring in different colors. This sow had two cubs that were cinnamon-colored. Having only come out of hibernation recently, they still have their thick winter coats.

Above: A bull moose searches for forage under the winter snow. Moose will drop their antlers in early January. The animals can be difficult to find in Yellowstone, though the northeast corner is always a good area to check in the winter. In the summer months, locating moose can be unpredictable.

Right: Winter snows blanket the Yellowstone region every winter. Lamar Valley becomes transformed into a winter wonderland, and the snow tells the story of every animal that passes through. In this instance, a red fox passed by on an early morning search for food.

Left: Pikas can be seen most commonly in the alpine and subalpine mountain areas. They are often heard before they are seen as they emit a loud squeak to warn of intruders.

Facing page: A channel of the Gallatin River flows under a stormy Yellowstone sky at sunset. The Gallatin River is one of three rivers that flows north and eventually forms the Missouri River. The Gallatin, like the Madison, has its headwaters in Yellowstone National Park. The stretch of the Gallatin through Yellowstone is some of the wildest parts of the park.

Below: The Lake Hotel is the oldest hotel in the National Park Service and is a National Historic Landmark. Originally opened in 1891 as a standard railroad hotel, it was later remodeled by Robert Reamer, the architect who designed the Old Faithful Inn, and has since undergone several remodels and additions. Today, the Colonial Revival-style hotel offers the simple, casual elegance of days gone by, with a string quartet that plays in the lobby during the summer months—and of course, spectacular views of Yellowstone Lake.

Left: Uinta ground squirrels are among the most common mammals in Yellowstone National Park. They hibernate in the winter and are only seen during the summer, when they're likely to run across the road as you're driving. These gregarious creatures can be found in almost any open meadow and are often misidentified as prairie dogs, which are not found in Yellowstone.

Far left: Firehole Cascades can be found along the one-way Firehole Canyon Drive. Since they are located upstream from the popular Firehole Falls and Firehole River swim area, many people miss these picturesque cascades as the river crashes through a narrow canyon.

Below: Long telephoto lenses of at least 500mm are required for photographing bears, and visitors should never approach a bear for any reason. When hiking in Yellowstone or the surrounding region, always carry bear spray. Everyone wants to see a bear, but make sure it's a safe experience.

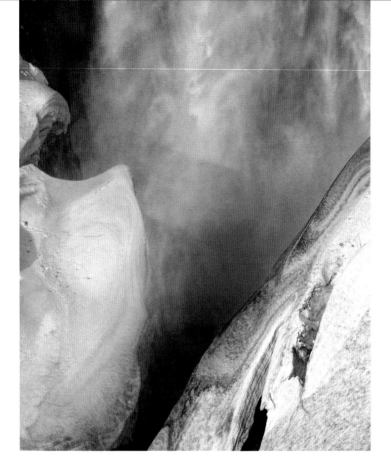

Above: Using a telephoto lens to create abstract images of Lower Falls can be fun and interesting. In the winter, a huge ice cone forms at the base of the falls, and a rainbow can be seen from multiple viewpoints at different times in the morning.

Right: The bitterroot is the state flower of Montana and blooms in the low elevations of Yellowstone in spring and early summer. The beautiful pink blossoms can be found growing in a variety of habitats, but it usually prefers dry soil.

Far right: An aurora borealis display in Yellowstone is a very rare occurrence, but when it does happen, it's a remarkable sight— especially when the northern lights are reflected in Great Fountain Geyser!

Above: For many visitors, sighting a great gray owl is a bucket list experience. These large owls can be two to three feet tall and have a wingspan of almost five feet. Owls are mostly nocturnal so are seldom seen, although they can occasionally be spotted in pine forests or hunting at the edge of a clearing.

Left: Chipmunks can be readily found in almost every picnic area in Yellowstone—in fact, if you sit still long enough, they'll probably find you first. Feeding even the smallest creatures in Yellowstone is against the rules, so don't do it, no matter how cute they may look.

Far left: A small log serves as a bridge over Daly Creek in Yellowstone's northwest corner. Some of the best hiking in the park is in this area, with incredible open scenery and abundant wildlife. Yellowstone has more than 900 miles of hiking trails, and it's hard to choose a bad one.

Right: With the right light, even something as common as Canada geese become magical. These geese decided to land along the Madison River at just the right moment, as the beautiful morning light provided a pinch of Yellowstone magic.

Far right: Green gentian can grow several feet in height and is common in open meadows in late summer. Seen here in early fall, the plant has already gone to seed. As morning mist rises from the Yellowstone River in Hayden Valley, the sun rises into a hazy Yellowstone sky.

Below: People find many different ways to enjoy Yellowstone. Hiking, fishing, or just seeing the sights and wildlife are all wonderful ways to spend time in the park. Many photographers come to Yellowstone in the hopes of capturing that once-in-a-lifetime moment, like this photographer walking along the Madison River at sunrise in search of that perfect photo.

Far left: Mount Sheridan can be seen in the distance from Fishing Bridge as the Yellowstone River leaves Yellowstone Lake. In this high-elevation plateau, winter is usually harsh and the snow can linger well into May, so the growing season for plant life only lasts a few months.

Left: Bald eagles can often be seen around bodies of water in the park. Look in treetops along rivers or at the edge of lakes and you might spot one as it watches for waterfowl or trout. As opportunists, they will also visit the carcass of a dead animal for an easy meal.

Below: After a mild winter, the snow in Yellowstone can melt quickly. But in a normal or severe winter, the snows will linger, especially if a cold spring follows. During this winter, Lake Lodge was still covered in snow in May since a normal winter was followed by a cold spring, and spring snows continued to add to the snow already on the ground.

Right: Coyote pups love to play, which makes them fun to watch. Coyotes will often den under a large tree root or a boulder and sometimes use the den dug out by another animal. They rarely reuse the same den and will often have several dug out nearby in case they need to move the pups.

Far right: Moose Falls is one of the first stops park visitors can make when entering Yellowstone from the south entrance. Often missed because the pullout isn't marked, it is worth finding to take the short path to view the thirty-foot falls as it plunges from Crawfish Creek.

Below: The Chocolate Pot is a hot spring found in an unmarked pullout along the Gibbon River. The name comes from the chocolate coloration of the hot spring caused by mineral oxides. Iron, aluminum, nickel, and other minerals are deposited from the hot spring. Notice the reddish coloration of the river bottom caused by the mineral deposits.

Above: Considered by many to be one of the best geyser shows in Yellowstone, Beehive Geyser can powerfully spray its water and steam up to a height of 200 feet and maintain it for approximately five minutes—and if you're lucky, you will see a rainbow in the fine mist. Beehive is one of the major geysers of the Upper Geyser Basin, and although it is not predictable like Old Faithful, a smaller geyser nearby, appropriately named Beehive's Indicator, often erupts shortly before Beehive, giving visitors enough warning to make it in time to see the big show.

Left: Late summer flowers and grasses are lit by the early morning sun at Fountain Flats. You may see bison here, or the occasional coyote, and you'll have a different view of the geysers at Lower Geyser Basin as they steam in the distance. Several thermal features can be found in the Lower Geyser Basin including geysers, fumaroles, springs, pools, and mud pots, with perhaps the main attraction being the Fountain Paint Pots, where boiling mud bubbles up from the ground.

Right: The red fox is one of three canines found in Yellowstone, along with the gray wolf and the coyote. As the smallest of the three, they are cautious and elusive. They are social animals and expert hunters.

Far right: Big Cone is a large sinter cone on the edge of Yellowstone Lake at the West Thumb Geyser Basin. While Big Cone has erupted in the past, it has only reached a height of about a foot. It's believed the flow of cold water from the lake into the cone keeps the water cool enough to limit eruptions, much like nearby Fishing Cone.

Below: Castle Geyser is named for the shape of its ancient cone, which resembles the ruins of an old castle. Because of its size and shape, Castle Geyser is very photogenic in many different types of light and conditions. Eruption predictions are posted in the visitor center, but the steam phase of the eruption is just as impressive as the water phase due to the roaring noise emitted by the geyser.

Above: Although this fawn seems to prefer a slow stroll among the wildflowers, the pronghorn is North America's fastest land mammal and can run at speeds up to fifty-five miles per hour. Fawns are born in June but, much like a deer fawn, will hide until they are strong enough to travel with their mothers.

Left: The fairy slipper, or calypso orchid, is one of the beauties of the forest found by lucky hikers in June. These lovely small orchids make great photo subjects, but since they are very sensitive to disturbance, it's extremely important to be careful not to disturb the habitat where the flowers are growing.

Far left: Wildflowers and summer go hand in hand, but spring rain and snow are critical to a good wildflower bloom. If May rains are plentiful, then June and July flowers should be too, as was the case when these flowers bloomed right off the road along Mary Bay. Much of this area is closed full-time for bear management purposes, so don't venture away from the road.

Above: Forest fires are a part of the delicate balance of nature in the Yellowstone ecosystem. Lodgepole pine trees cover a vast majority of the landscape. Adapted to fire, the lodgepole actually needs fire to help it reproduce. It has two different types of pine cones; one of these, called a serotinous cone, is closed and requires extreme heat to open so it can release its seeds.

Right: Badgers are a common animal to Yellowstone, yet are rarely seen. These master diggers are usually burrowing underground for their preferred prey, ground squirrels. But even when they are above ground, they blend in so well with the surrounding sagebrush that they are well camouflaged. Sometimes the best way to spot a badger is by the dirt flying while it's digging—but keep your distance—badgers can be as fierce as their wolverine cousins.

Facing page: Tower Fall is located in the north section of Yellowstone along the Grand Loop Road. At 132 feet tall, it is one of the park's primary attractions, popular in both summer and winter. A large parking area with nearby campground and general store is provided, along with a paved trail that leads to an overlook.

Above: Gray wolves can come in a variety of colors and mixed shades of white, black, brown, and gray—but all wolves will lighten as they age. Several wolves in Yellowstone that were black as youngsters are now very light. The alpha female of the Canyon pack, seen on the right, has become much lighter as she aged and is now almost completely white, much as her mother before her.

Left: Snowshoe hares turn white in the winter and don't turn brown again until sometime in the spring. They're easier to spot in the early spring by keeping an eye open for the "running ball of snow," as they often still have their winter coloration even after the snow melts. The name "snowshoe" comes from their large hind legs, which make them highly mobile in winter conditions.

Far left: A small cascade on the Gibbon River is blanketed in a late spring snow. One of the beauties of Yellowstone is that many hidden treasures are located along the Grand Loop Road. At one time these spots may have been appreciated by more visitors, but have been lost over time. Travel in the early days of the park was often by stagecoach, so having interesting places to stop and stretch was welcome, and places like this may have been a good choice. Today, many people speed through the park not knowing what hidden gems they pass by.

Above: The sky takes on incredible color as the sun rises over a frozen Gallatin River. The best sunrises happen when the low horizon is clear, but high clouds can be seen in the sky. Winters are severe in Yellowstone, and on a morning such as this when temperatures are well below zero, dressing in warm layers—complete with head covering, good boots, and gloves—is a must.

Right: The American marten, commonly referred to as a pine marten, is a common resident in the forests of Yellowstone. These cat-sized predators are extremely agile, and are solitary creatures, except during the breeding season in August. Kits are born during the winter and will stay with the mother until autumn. Very elusive and mostly nocturnal, they are rarely seen by park visitors—so if you do spot one, it is a rare treat. I spotted this marten as it was resting in a pine tree.

Far right: Clepsydra Geyser, Greek for "water clock," can be seen in the Lower Geyser Basin. Since the 1959 Hebgen earthquake, Clepsydra erupts almost constantly, only pausing for a minute or so before it continues its playful eruptions. This makes it a reliable subject for a dramatic sunrise or sunset photo.

Above: A pronghorn buck makes a handsome portrait. Pronghorn can be seen on any of the open sage flats in the park, with Lamar Valley being a great place to look. Early morning or late afternoon are best, but pronghorn can be spotted at any time of day.

Left: Bison are commonly seen grazing on Fountain Flats, and when the temperatures are cool, large steam plumes from geysers make for an "only-in-Yellowstone" background.

Facing page: Electric Peak is the tallest peak in the Gallatin Range of southern Montana, rising to a height of 10,969 feet above sea level. It is visible from many places in Yellowstone, but the best views are from Swan Lake Flat. Beautiful any time of year, Electric Peak takes on a special beauty when covered in snow.

Right: A bull elk pursues a cow during the September elk rut on an early misty morning. Photographing bull elk backlit in the morning mist is one of my favorite photo opportunities. Elk are abundant in the park and can most often be seen in the early morning or late afternoon.

Far right: There's no bad time to experience Yellowstone, though early morning walks allow for a little more solitude. The boardwalk at West Thumb leads directly by Black Pool, which, at thirty feet deep, is one of the largest hot pools at West Thumb. The water temperature is 132 degrees and provides a lot of misty steam, especially on cool mornings.

Below: Fly-fishing is one of the popular ways to spend time in Yellowstone, and the Madison River is considered one of the best fly-fishing rivers in the country. In fact, fishing enthusiasts come from all over the world to cast a fly here.

Left: Moose calves are born each spring in late May, but may not be seen until June. They stay with their mother for a year, and a cow will fiercely protect her young.

Far left: Mystic Falls is a popular hiking destination in the Old Faithful area. A short hike from the Biscuit Basin boardwalk leads to this seventy-foot waterfall. Care should be taken if exploring around the waterfall, as several small thermal features seep scalding hot water out of the canyon walls. The trail continues up the hillside above the falls and loops back to the start point with some nice views along the way.

Below: Grizzlies are very protective of their young. This sow grizzly was comforting her cub after it was scared by the loud noise of a passing truck.

Above: River otters frequent many of the waterways in Yellowstone National Park and are commonly spotted around Yellowstone Lake and the Yellowstone River. They may be seen alone or in small family groups, like this family of otters affectionately grooming each other.

Right: Asters are one of the last wildflowers to bloom across Yellowstone, and it's not uncommon for these beautiful purple flowers to wait to bloom until the first snow falls in September.

Far right: Lupine are one of the more common wildflowers seen during the summer months, as they bloom in a wide variety of places. Hayden Valley often has beautiful displays of lupine in June.

Next pages: Great Fountain Geyser is a fountain-type geyser that usually erupts to around 100 feet, but can have eruptions that burst up to 200 feet in height. Its sinter platform is so pretty that even when not erupting, it's a beautiful sight, especially at sunset.

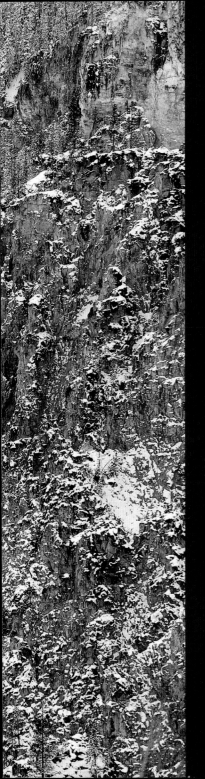

Above: With deep snow covering much of the interior of Yellowstone, many bison use the roads to travel since it's much easier and requires less energy expenditure, which is important in the lean, cold months. While out in the park one cold day in February, I caught this image of three bull bison walking along a snowpacked road. They were only in this perfect symmetry for one moment; the very next frame—less than a second later—that perfect moment was gone. This is one of my favorite images, which I call "Three Amigos." It was displayed in the Smithsonian Institution National Museum of Natural History in 2008.

Left: Lower Falls as viewed from Artist Point on the South Rim is one of the most iconic scenes of Yellowstone. Coming away with a photo that's a little bit different from the typical postcard image is a challenge a photographer cannot resist, and often requires a bit of luck. On this spring morning, an early snow added a different dimension to an already beautiful scene, as a soft light cast warm tones over the beautiful snow-touched details of the majestic Grand Canyon of the Yellowstone.

Next page: A lone bull elk walks along the Madison River at sunrise. Elk are the most numerous large mammal found in Yellowstone. Although common throughout the Northern Rockies, no sound can compare to the hauntingly beautiful bugle of a bull elk on a cool September morning in Yellowstone.

STEPHEN C. HINCH

Award-winning photographer Steve Hinch is a full-time resident in West Yellowstone. What was supposed to be one summer in Yellowstone has become more than a decade of living and working in the Yellowstone/ Grand Teton area.

Through his wildlife and landscape images from across the country, Hinch shares unique views of nature as they happened in that moment in time. Hinch's images have been featured in a variety of publications and collections, including the Smithsonian Institution National Museum of Natural History.

To see more of Steve Hinch's photography, visit www.stevehinchphotography.com.